D1724969

Conscious
Dinner
Parties

Conscious Dinner Parties

A Girlfriend's Guide *to* 9 Transformational Gatherings

JYL AUXTER

BALBOA
PRESS

A DIVISION OF HAY HOUSE

The book has been edited by Sangeet Duchane.

Balboa Press books may be ordered through booksellers or by contacting:

Balboa Press
A Division of Hay House
1663 Liberty Drive
Bloomington, IN 47403
www.balboapress.com
1-(877) 407-4847

ISBN: 978-1-4525-7559-9 (sc)
ISBN: 978-1-4525-7557-5 (hc)
ISBN: 978-1-4525-7558-2 (e)

Printed in the United States of America.

Balboa Press rev. date: 06/24/2013

To Malala Yousafzai, the young Pakistani girl who was shot by Taliban militant while on her way to school. As Malala speaks out for women's rights, let her work be powerfully felt around the world.

TABLE OF CONTENTS

GIRLFRIEND GIFT

The Conscious Dinner Parties book is a gift for my beloved (your friend's name)

_____

Presented (date & time) _____

You're a special girlfriend (because) _____

_____

_____

_____

Love (your name) _____

Congratulation! You're invited to a Conscious Dinner Party.

Date _____   Time _____

Location _____

Hello Girlfriends!

Today, women around the world are waking up to a profound shift in consciousness. Now more than ever, we are seeking conscious connections and balance to hectic lives as we heal the planet—one girlfriend at a time. I personally want to thank every woman who shares the *Conscious Dinner Parties* book with her friends. It is time to party with a purpose while celebrating our womanhood and priceless friendships. Honor and love every girlfriend because she is a precious creature and a true reflection of our own inner beauty.

In my heart, I know this book is life enhancing. It might seem to be something else on the *To Do* list, but if embraced, the insights revealed are sure to save later on doctor bills, appointments with the therapist and hours on the phone dealing with girlfriend dramas. The powerful dining affairs offered by this tome have been designed to help all of us look and feel healthier. Each event reveals healing insights into our own psyches with plenty of female playtime to make the journey fun.

Let's face it, women love any reason to get together and share. We will use any excuse to buy a new pair of shoes and celebrate. I say put on the lipstick and grab a tiara because it is time to cook up some excitement at the *Conscious Dinner Parties*. Discover your true nature in the company of favorite friends. Be the best girlfriend in this life and surround yourself with other spiritually conscious women. Nothing is more important than creating time to nurture healthy relationships and share the love.

Blessings & Gratitude,
Jyl Auxter

INTRODUCTION

The mystery of consciousness lies within the duality of life itself... The question we must continually ask ourselves is how do we co-exist with a calming spiritual realm and yet maintain a powerful earthly life experience?

A Girlfriend's Guide to *Conscious Dinner Parties* is an entertaining book written for conscious, seeking women of all ages who love to learn, grow and spend time in their kitchens. A riveting keepsake, this rite of passage is the perfect house gift, serving as an innocent teaching tool for spiritual and personal transformation. Please, don't mistake *transformation* for religious dogma, Wiccan practices or radical feminism. Serious but subtle shifts are on the horizon as women begin to live from their hearts. Think of the impact this will have on the world as women step into their power and transition into a higher level of consciousness.

A distinct book for its time, *Conscious Dinner Parties* will dazzle and inspire the chef in the kitchen as she is given permission to create delicious, sustainable and healing foods for her first Metaphysical dinner party. Learn a mystic's approach to cooking and organizing seven transformational dining affairs plus two mystery events. Girlfriends can take turns in the kitchen creating a true union of souls with rituals that can be celebrated by all cultures and religions. The time is now to change from old, worn out customs and beliefs to exciting new age modes.

Conscious dinners are home-based parties that guide women and their daughters toward balanced life choices, a sense of self, better health and stronger female friendships. Now which comrades are lucky enough to be invited? All concerns are covered in the book, from which girlfriends to invite, the perfect dish to serve and entertaining ideas for learning a savory life lesson. Discuss love, power and lusty desires, all topics of great importance to women.

Delighted by such an insightful and arousing creation, women and their daughters throughout the world will buy several books to always have available as the perfect house gift.

Part I

Party Preparations

DEFINE CONSCIOUSNESS

Unplug from life for a precious night out with the girls. This fast-paced world, driven by technology, has completely redefined our lives and the way we communicate with our girlfriends. In these inspiring times of a digital age, iPhones and iPads have governed our days, keeping us quite busy—some would say unconsciously busy—Skyping, Twittering and checking hourly Facebook feeds. The Internet has made it easier to download a quick movie on iTunes instead of running out with a friend for buttery popcorn and a big-screen flick.

Think back to the days when there was extra time to sit and chat over a steamy hot latte or cup of exotic tea. Something has happened to our lives and personal time. Technology, demanding work schedules and family obligations must not limit us from quality girlfriend time and a chance for personal growth. For busy women, this is a sign to stop and schedule a conscious moment. Give a book to friends and offer an unbreakable commitment to a lifetime of sacred sisterhood.

> *Attention: Women have a mission to awaken and by doing so will teach and love this planet back to a balanced place. More applications are needed to ground conscious living into the world and this book gives females permission to get started.*

The word *consciousness* is a mouthful of an overused label that is being thrown around by the media, authors and new age gurus. Yet, do we truly understand this declaration and what it means or how it may impact our daily lives? Why is consciousness so important during these current times? What is a conscious dinner party? How can an innocent diner teach us the importance of healing and leading a spiritually whole and meaningful life?

Let's start by defining the word conscious. English dictionaries tend to refer to a person as either dead or no longer conscious or consciously alive. William James, a noted American psychologist, compared the conscious mind to a stream; unbroken and continuous despite constant shifts and changes. The importance of this concept has been studied for centuries. Since the '90s the new age movement has taken this word out of a limiting definition and brought it into the powerful present-tense application. We are now living in a conscious period where we have learned to cook consciously, eat consciously, consciously become aware of the global warming and to meditate to become more conscious.

The definition to be used in this context is "Conscious" as an adjective. Aware of what one is doing, feelings and thinking either deliberate or intentional action linked with spiritual insights.

Up to now conscious eating or cooking were code words for learning how to become Vegan or Raw. This book is not going to preach food faddist methods. Be prepared to receive spiritual truths, healing rituals and slow-food dining instructions. Since we are spiritual beings by nature, why not intentionally be available for a real nurturing and a divine healing event? It is time to try something new. Cook up some magic and fall into a transformational night. Gone are the days of pop psychology on the telephone as we coach our girlfriend with her latest drama. It's time to hang up the phones, turn off the computers and gift ourselves a party. Conscious dinner and tea parties are the latest girlie gatherings promoting personal development and sisterly love.

Don't mistake a spiritually conscious gathering for a religious experience. The benevolent super-beings represented in Jesus, Buddha,

Rumi and others have all shown the way to greater Truths. Jesus created a conscious dining affair by hosting the Last Supper. Buddha most likely enjoyed royal conscious dinners with his family before setting out to sit under the Bodhi tree and Rumi probably enjoyed a sustainable feast with conscious acquaintances after whirling with his dervishes. Now it is our turn. The conscious dinner parties will celebrate the union of all souls, regardless of religious and cultural beliefs. These parties promote peace on earth by bringing love into the homes of all brave hostesses. Share laughs and healthy recipes. The only requirement is for women to show up real and take a turn in the kitchen then post the fun on Facebook.

Right about now some of you might be thinking, "I can remember a couple wild parties where drinking double and thinking single were the dinner themes, followed by an infuriated husband and a nasty hangover." We have all been to those parties where we thought a drink or two could help us fit in and feel more comfortable. Then there were the parties where we ate ourselves into a tizzy and the next day said those famous last words, "I will never do that again!" Think back to unconscious parties of the past: loud and out of control, stuffy and boring, unimpressive and never-ending. Times are changing and so are the standards for sensitive contemplative females and the events these women choose to attend.

Nine is a powerful number representing transformation. The first seven dinner parties are carefully designed. Each offers basic tools to assist the women as they awaken an inner knowingness. The last two dinner parties present a test, as the hostess is asked to fill in the blanks and start designing one of two mystery dinners. Has the message really been absorbed? Soon it will be clear if the hostess is consciously capable or must re-read and ponder some of the pages.

As we step into our kitchens, we can be the first in the neighborhood to learn a mystic's approach to cooking and organizing a special affair. Transition and launch girlfriends from old worn-out customs and beliefs to an updated, healthier lifestyle. Let's get ready to liberate our girlie selves. Soul sisters join together and prepare to open the inside of our minds, kitchens and hearts. It's time to party with a purpose.

CREATE CONSCIOUS GATHERINGS

Consciousness—please don't let this mouthful of a word be intimidating. There is reason why the expression has become popular with so many of us today. People actually want to wake up and live more passionately. This phrase pushes us to inquire more. Lately, we have started to ask ourselves big life questions concerning the effectiveness of our current government systems, the safety of our food and water, healthcare methods, sustainable banks, job opportunities and qualified schools for our children. The time has come to understand the ramifications of global warming, lack of gun control and the safety of our planet. The next vital question becomes, "What will my conscious contribution be to the world?" This tough interrogation will surely motivate and guide us to make sensible personal changes for future growth.

A transformation is needed to insure a joyful existence. It is time to fill ourselves up with delight and put our energies where they really matter—with our beloved girlfriends. Learn to live a healthier life and grow spiritually. Let's get real and conscious as we learn to slow down and appreciate the moment. Take one night off from social media, family duties, draining careers and other distractions to rouse some inner truths. It is time to regain our spiritual nature, show our strengths and live as conscious women.

Paradigm shifts are occurring throughout the planet. The word paradigm simply means our overriding belief systems are changing. To be real and conscious means we are now making it a priority to join our sisters, old acquaints, mothers, daughters and new friends for a sacred event. Break routines from old beliefs and try something new. It might feel uncomfortable at first, but just do it. Getting conscious means gladly going along with a new protocol as we learn to calm the fears and stay in our hearts.

Breathe: Before reading further, take a few moments to reflect. Settle into a comfy chair and take a deep inhale followed by a slow exhale breath. Think about the following questions: What is a spiritual journey? What does the word conscious mean in regards to a spiritual journey? How does being spiritual differ from being religious? What does it mean to live a life of grace? What pain is in the body? What is the core cause of major worries?

Grab a piece of paper and do some journaling. Stay conscious— focused on the here and now. As thoughts come up, notice which emotions are surfacing and in what areas of the body. These will be important details for the life lessons later during the parties, but for now just become mindful and jot down noted discoveries.

In this very moment, the union of all people is the sacred message. *Can we learn to get along?* This is our contemporary battle cry. The concept of *separateness* is very outdated and not a viable way to live. The *it's all about greedy little me* times are long gone. We need each other to get the job done and clean up this world. We need our soul sisters to be spiritually awakened and conscious so we can start promoting the message to our children, husbands, grandchildren and the rest of the world.

It starts with busy women in their kitchens. Let's face it; gals are always in the kitchen even if they don't cook. Right? In spiritual terms, the master teacher would feed her students ancient transcendent knowledge. The spiritual energy that women come by naturally will be the force to break this world wide open. It is time to be a conscious woman and help shift the planet. Women will teach the world that foods are meant to heal, that *G-O-D* and *J-O-Y* are really safe three-letter words and the time has come to embrace a new mantra—love and compassion for all people.

In order to live mindfully, the first job on the agenda is to heal and clear any disappointments of the past. Wounds of not being good enough may still be hidden away like a messy sock drawer. It is time to tidy up. It is okay to be vulnerable and shed some tears as we stay true to the journey of a warrior. As our pasts are cleared, the path becomes unblocked and the energy vibrant. We are able to understand our purpose for being on this planet. Our conscious responsibility is to start teaching our daughters that real power is within the heart and soul, not in breast implants or collagen lips. Thin is not always in! Let's stop starving ourselves and start healing as we show up for active duties in our kitchens.

Being in the present moment means that we feel good in our skins and we have the courage to empower other women to feel the same way. The scan-and-compare technique as we pass our fellow women on the sidewalk must stop if we are going to become world leaders. We are perfect creatures. Thinner, cuter, smarter, richer, healthier and happier are illusions that must not be passed down to the next generation.

Women are we ready? Are we prepared to get real and heal our lives with this book? Each dinner party will offer a noticeable energetic shift. This alteration will come as a magical transformation as we begin to feel remarkably different in our bodies. This change will be recognizable by the ninth party as we see behavioral differences in ourselves and the other girls. We are going to have a complete makeover without new makeup. It is time to prepare for a grand opportunity and a healthy revolution.

How to use the book

K itchen consciousness is one of the main themes when hosting a healthy event. Is the food sustainable and medicine for the body? The *Conscious Dinner Parties* are opportunities for girlfriends to use their homes as ashrams and laboratories for better living. The following is a list of dinner parties to be created. Customize these healing soirees to fit the needs of the guests:

> The Survival Kit Party
> The Play and Passion Party
> The Power and Truth Party
> The Love Feast Party
> The Heaven on Earth Party
> The Intuitive Dinner Party
> The Live Joy Dinner Party
> The First Mystery Dinner Party
> The Second Mystery Dinner Party

As a gift

Use this book as a gift. Girlfriends are always buying each other little tokens of love and appreciation. A beautiful book is a remnant that brings an immediate flashback of fond memories. Throughout time, the *Conscious Dinner Parties* book will be a reliable source for learning sacred messages. This is truly a gift that will

never be outdated and can be passed down to future generations. Share the love when gifting this book and only the deepest affections shall be returned.

To host a party buy eight books as presents for girlfriends. Think of anyone who has been forgotten on your gift list—Christmas, birthdays or anniversaries. It is time to visit and gift a *Conscious Dinner Parties* book. Make sure to beautifully wrap it with a signature style. Consider a bow of brightly colored ribbon and fresh-picked flowers from the garden.

Before giftwrapping, make sure to fill in the empty blanks on the front page. This area is for writing an uplifting message followed by a loving signature. If the book is an invitation for a dinner event, offer a specific date and time for the upcoming party. If however it is not a gift for dinner or the details have not been decided upon, leave the blanks empty. Present the book to friends within a couple of weeks to ensure a flow of excitement among the xx chromosome cronies. Then go ahead, Skype, Facebook and Twitter the girls and include the time and date for the first magical involvement.

The girlfriend who has gifted the books will host the first party. She is the royal queen in charge of organizing a majestic event just perfect for all her noble friends. If for some reason this never happens—queens do get busy in their kingdoms, then any girl, whether she has received the book as a gift or has purchased her own copy, can start the process. It will be the hostess's responsibility to assign one dinner to each girlfriend or she can decide that her guests can volunteer for a specific dinner of their choice. The parties will be a monthly celebration. It is very important to keep a steady flow to insure a positive momentum with the gals. If lack of money or location becomes a problem, be creative and pray. The angels will inspire resolutions.

As a learning tool

The book offers everything from recipes to healing instructions. Stay true to the themes but be creative and make these soirees ones to remember. Discover decorating tips, the perfect outfits and music suggestions to create a dreamy environment with a higher healing vibration. Add essential oils for that new-age restorative effect. Be bold and invite professionals to share their knowledge. These experts might include: favorite teachers, musicians, yoga gurus, therapists and holistic healers. This is a sure way to grow a conscious community in the neighborhoods.

While the immediate focus will be on the general hosting instructions, shortly the conscious life lessons will become the featured highlight of every party. Each gal is required to roll up her sleeves and participate by becoming vulnerable to any personal emotional leftovers. These life lessons will empower the guests and chef to stay motivated with each party. In the end, all the gatherings will offer the girlfriends great insights about themselves and each other.

As a game

By the end of the ninth party, the group will vote on a lucky woman to be awarded the most, Conscious Contributor. This is the woman who thoroughly understands the principals of the conscious life lessons and has applied them to her life. A second prize goes to the most improved. This is the gal who might have come kicking and screaming to the parties but in the end was completely accepting of the message and was profoundly impacted. The third award goes to the best overall house party. This is the girl who went out of her way to creatively fuss for her friends, and at the same time was committed to reading the book and following the suggested party themes.

As the nine gatherings get assembled, stay conscious and contribute wisely. Although only three prizes have been mentioned, it is acceptable to arrange more. Let the consensus of the group govern the ultimate number of game prizes to be endowed. Let the girlfriends decide upon the prizes. Will the accolades be a certificate to hang on the wall or a bouquet of flowers? The success of the prizes will depend on the inventiveness of the group.

Invite Girlfriends

Who will be invited?

S ummon nine (includes the hostess) lucky friends and/or family members to the dinner parties who are in desperate need of a hall pass from life's chaos. It is time to recharge the batteries and grow spiritually. It just takes one gal to kick off this event as she assumes the duties of the hostess and buys books to gift her companions. Then for the next nine months, girlfriends will cook, play and develop into strong-spirited leaders. The ladies will return home after each event breeding consciousness into their families and friends.

Girlfriends are mirror inner-reflections and much needed today for self-discovery. We unconsciously manifest each other to form an evolving soul-group to learn strengths and weaknesses. This means if there are mother issues or problems with emotional boundaries, these reflections will be stored somewhere inside our favorite friend just waiting for the precise opportunity to be revealed. This becomes a grand synchronicity to surrender and grow. It will take courage to look inside ourselves and love what we find.

Who should be invited to join the group as the planning begins and the consciousness flows? Invite from the following suggested list:

A childhood friend with history
A brand-new friend
A workout buddy
A spiritual or religious friend
A younger friend
An older friend
A spouse's friend
A nurturing friend
A mother, stepmother, daughter, stepdaughter
A sister, stepsister, niece, cousin, grandmother, step-grandmother
A current best friend
An acquaintance needing support, healing or love
BE BOLD. Ask a difficult girlfriend

With each invitation be excited about the uncertainty and magic that lies ahead. The parties will take on exceptional energies based on the invitees and their contributions and dedication. The goal for each girl is to stay open and accepting. Anytime more than one person gets involved there will be dynamics. **Group dynamics** may affect a gal's willingness to be unguarded and receiving—this is how we grow. There will be many personalities and they may bring along their baggage, and I don't mean a Louis Vuitton. It will now become important for the hostess of each party to assign a behind-the-scene mediator. This is a person who values fairness and can take control if necessary. If intense unattractive emotions begin to arise, it is time for the intermediary to step in and save the day. In some cases, there may be one gal who needs to control or comes to the party full of negative energies. Prayers, hugs and healthy boundaries work well to alter the energies before the evening gets out of control. In case that fails, bring in the mediator.

Intention

The word *intention* means a course of action a person intends to follow. It is the determination to act a certain way or to achieve a certain goal. Setting clear intentions for each party is by far the best way to secure happy and healthy participants. This is a great approach to insure successful parties. For instance, the intentions set by this book are: *to create significant spiritual shifts, awaken the unconscious, empower women on the planet to live peacefully and from their highest potential.* The hostess and guests will need to set clear intentions for each of the nine events. The stronger the intentions, the greater the impact this will have on the ladies.

Tips for a successful party

I t is important to have structure for these monthly celebrations. The tips will include helpful suggestions for kitchen duties, organizing the spiritual lessons and rituals and the perfect closure to a magical evening. Keep the expectations low and remember less is more. Less drama with more heart energy is the goal for the finest outcome. Be clear to set a powerful intention before heading to the kitchen and then again as buddies are ringing the doorbell—think blessings and be grateful for this unique experience with friends. Don't forget to videotape or take photos for the Twitter after-party crowd.

Kitchen tips

1. Always show respect for guests by asking in advance what food allergies or food dislikes exist within the group.
2. Think sustainable, buy organic and support the local farmer. Limit processed foods by thinking fresh, clean and homegrown. Be bold and create a garden of healthy organic fruits, vegetables, herbs and flowers, then share with friends.
3. Cook and infuse love into the food by praying, laughing, singing, setting a healing intention or simply placing hands directly above the food and saying, *love, love, love.*
4. Essential oils now become a conscious item on the menu and are taken out of the cosmetic, *smell good only* category. If the oil is therapeutic grade, place a couple drops directly into the food for flavor. This creates a new vibration and spices up any old dish.
5. It is most important to keep the dinners light, nutritious—pure and simple.

Lesson and ritual tips

1. Remember, the guest list will be filled with women who are curious about spiritual truths and are hungry for joy in their lives. Each guest will return the favor of being gifted a book and will host a party.

2. All dinner parties will include an opening and closing spiritual ritual. Here are a few examples of rituals: ringing of Tibetan bells, chanting, singing, secret handshakes, hugs, lighting candles and an energy protection prayer.

3. Invite holistic healers, yogis and spiritual teachers to the parties. Let these experts share their knowledge in exchange for a marketing opportunity and a memorable meal.

4. After dinner, let the games begin by forming a sacred circle to discuss the conscious life lesson, the healing ritual; then meditate. Make sure to leave plenty of time for discussion after each exercise.

5. No angry voices or jealous rages are to be added to the party themes. No gossip or negative chitchat.

6. Very important: The intention has been set to a higher spiritual vibration. Unfortunately, alcohol, cigarettes, drugs, bad-quality food and negative energies are of a lower frequency and do not blend well with this affair—be cautious.

7. Don't be afraid to use incense, candles and therapeutic-grade essential oils. Create the perfect sanctuary.

8. Be gentle with each other as the conscious life lessons are discussed. Allow each girl to have the freedom to share strengths and weaknesses without heavy judgments. Nurture any tears and open the heart to receive loving feedback. Remember, there are no rights and wrongs. Let everyone's voice be heard, and please keep in mind that no one has been

granted permission to play therapist, life coach or Dr. Phil. These are spiritual events with angels and spirit guides as the counseling body in charge of peace.

Closing party tips

1. Girlfriends need to be reading the book to keep up with the flow of events and the upcoming teachings.
2. Make sure all dinner parties end with love. Save extra moments for hugs and kisses.
3. Make sure the next event has been organized with a date, time, location and an assigned hostess.
4. Burn a sage stick or spray a sage mist (9 drops of sage oil into a small 2-ounce spray container of purified water) into the air after the event to clear the energy once the evening has ended.
5. After each party, always take a bath in Epson salt and apple cider vinegar before going to bed. This will cut all connections to the group and will insure a peaceful sleep.
6. What has been learned from the experience? Save a few minutes to journal. Write to clear the clutter from the mind, creating room for peace and a good night's sleep.
7. If for some reason friends can't gather during the evening hours then Saturday afternoon tea or a Sunday brunch will work just fine.

Party Preparations

P reparing for the party will require some skills. Most of us have to coordinate this activity with busy family duties, overwhelming work schedules and unexpected daily occurrences. Once a party has been assigned, let the planning begin. Allow enough time for the following: grocery shopping (*a couple of days before the event*), prepping and lightly precooking the food (*early afternoon of the party*), setting the table (*the night before*), decorating the dining room (*the day before*), organizing the life lesson and healing ritual (*delegate or organize a couple of weeks prior to date of the party*) and a self-healing catnap (*three hours before party*). Note that the pre-party, self-healing catnap is a requirement.

Please shop at organic local farmer's markets or sustainable grocery stores. Demand organic foods for conscious dinners and for every meal served. Around the world, health food stores offer many fresh vegetables and sustainable meats along with natural healing products. Learn to change habits and buy healthy merchandise. Be assured this action alone will shift our world and rid us of many unnecessary health problems.

If cooking is not a talent of yours then keep the meal simple or invite a friend to help out in the kitchen. Think easy and design a plate with yummy breads, crackers, cheeses, fresh fruits and vegetables—nibble all night long. A hearty soup is uncomplicated and doesn't require much time to prepare. These parties should not be hard work. On the other hand, please avoid calling out for pizza. The guests will appreciate all the labor that goes into the evening.

If you love to cook then show off! Just possibly the life lesson will take the group back into the kitchen for a *healing with foods* cooking demonstration. Be an example for the others and let the culinary talents flow. Remember to call in the angels while cooking. This will shift the energies in the kitchen, the meal and all who partake in this sacred ceremony.

Pre-dinner checklist

- ✓ Plan menu around the suggested theme
- ✓ Groccry shop—think organic and local
- ✓ Make sure to note any foods to be avoided
- ✓ Include friends to help with the cooking or go solo
- ✓ Prep food to reheat and serve upon guests' arrival
- ✓ Have non-alcoholic beverage ready to serve in fussy chilled goblets

- ✓ Organize the life lesson, healing ritual or delegate
- ✓ Remember to take a self-healing catnap!

Directions for self-healing catnap

Make sure to set an alarm clock, as we wouldn't want to miss the party.

Lie down on a bed and get comfortable. Begin to take deep inhale and exhale breaths.

Place hands over closed eyes and use a pillow under elbows for support. Continue to breathe and relax.

After about five minutes, allow the hands to move to the side of the head by the ears. Stay for the same amount of time then remove the pillow and position the hands gently behind the neck.

Wait another five minutes and then move the hands to the chest. Notice how the body is starting to melt into a deeper state of relaxation. Bring the hands to the naval area and feel the feet. Finally, place the hands on the hips.

Most likely sleep will have overcome the body at some point so upon awakening, feel refreshed and ready to be the impeccable hostess.

PART II

Let the Parties Begin

Below is a reminder of the nine parties to will be assigned:

1. The Survival Kit Party—time to ground back into the body
2. The Play and Passion Party—the freedom to play
3. The Power and Truth Party—emotional, mental and spiritual gym work
4. The Love Feast Party—cherub emotional clearings
5. The Heaven on Earth Party—chitchat paddy whack
6. The Intuitive Dinner Party—white witches and broomsticks
7. The Live Joy Dinner Party—angel intervention
8. The First Mystery Dinner Party—holistically whole
9. The Second Mystery Dinner Party—divinely designed

Each party is comprised of the following 11 elements: a party overview, conscious life lesson, higher and lower aspects of character, healing ritual, musical vibration, color theme, essential oils, meditation, closing ceremony, after party ritual and conscious fortune cookie message. The following descriptions explain each party element in more detail.

Overview

The overview is simply a black-and-white snapshot of the party to be hosted and provides an overall feeling for the night. A sample menu, one recipe, decorating tips and table settings are revealed in each party overview. Decorating colors are mentioned as the menu is planned and outfits are considered.

Keep in mind that the sample menu offers plenty of food ideas. Not every item needs to be prepared. Maybe serving a starter and the main dish is just too much food for the gals. All final decisions are left up to the hostess. Recipes for most of menu ideas can be found in *What's Cooking Within*, an Ayurveda and Yoga cookbook. This cookbook can be purchased at www.jylauxter.com.

Conscious life lesson

The conscious life lessons are key components to teaching mindfulness and spirituality. Each dinner party has a conscious theme. These themes help us make sense of life when chaos hits. We often tend to judge actions and ourselves as good or bad, right or wrong, instead of considering that both parts of these sets of character traits define us and are always changing. We can learn a great deal about ourselves and our journeys by contemplating each conscious moment.

Higher and lower aspects

We start each dining affair by discussing how we can consciously become in charge of our lives by allowing the higher aspects to lead our attention. This means we are acutely aware of ourselves when we drop into the lower aspects or our weaknesses. Without creating a drama, we learn to use this self-awareness technique to generate inner peace, observe what is going on in our lives and quickly shift our energy as we get back on a positive track. Over time, if we maintain a strong focus on our strengths instead of weaknesses, we are able to form a new habit. From time to time, harsh stresses push lower aspects back into our lives, and we discover how horribly uncomfortable it feels. We have become consciously aware of a new healthy pattern. Congratulations!

Gone are the days to simply abandon girlfriends. Life lessons offer a balanced solution to all of our friends when emotional weaknesses show up. We give ourselves adequate time to reframe bad behaviors and immediately become aware of another choice. Instead of dwelling on weaknesses or spending time resisting, quickly become conscious and focus on strengths. During the conscious cosmic parties, use the other women to better define and simplify strengths and weaknesses. Learn to stay positive with all communications: emails, personal conversations, inner dialogs. Soon astonishing shifts will begin to occur in life.

Healing ritual

The word *ritual* can conjure up a plentitude of images. Religious ceremonies during church on Sunday mornings might be the most familiar rituals. Another example is a Hindu prayer before starting a yoga practice. Believe it or not, a simple handshake and a gesture of hello can be considered a ritual. A ritual is simply a set of actions performed mainly for symbolic value with the purpose of strengthening a bond between people.

Healthy rituals seem to have lost their importance in our culture, and it's time to reconnect with some important rites of passage in order to grow spiritually. The role of rituals in *Conscious Dinner Parties* is to offer a social action aimed at creating a transformation that moves a woman into a higher level of awareness about herself. These higher vibrational parties help create conscious version of ourselves and our beloved friends. Thus, a sacred ritual creates spiritual women.

A healing ritual connects girlfriends to their inner-core essence, forcing growth. These dinner parties offer the time to dig deep and find a spiritual sweet spot. As these energies are accessed, a major connection will be established between friends and the spirit world. By design, the presence of this collective consciousness offers a magical and transformational gathering to take place that can be felt by everyone.

Meditation or the neutral mind

Meditation is a ritual to be included at every dinner. The group will co-create an extraordinary experience through meditation. Simply close the eyes to connect spiritually, then breathe and stay present. Allow thoughts to gently come and go as you learn to create a neutral space within the mind. Go inward to feel the powerful energy of spirit. The ability to meditate will become stronger and stronger with every dining affair. A neutral mind or spiritual connection is obtained through meditation. This bond will be deeply valued by the end of the ninth party because of the peace and insights it offers. Everyone will become clearer on what it truly means to settle the mind and go into a deliberate place of joy.

Eventually, through meditation our consciousness grows. Over time we begin to notice that focusing on the duality of higher and lower aspects of character will begin to fade in its importance. Our neurotic thinking minds have surrendered into a peaceful and more neutral place within. We no longer desire to identify with the duality and prefer to love what it happening in the moment. This is an advanced approach to living a conscious life. This concept becomes much clearer as we embark upon the dinner parties and our sacred journeys.

Samadhi is a spiritual experience that occurs during advanced states of meditation. The meanings for this Sanskrit word, *Samadhi*, in Hinduism, Buddhism, Jainism, Sikhism and yogic schools all represent the same truth: a higher level of concentration or *dhyāna*. In the yogic tradition, *dhyāna* is the eighth and final limb identified in the Yoga Sūtras of Patañjali (yogi's bible). Samadhi has been described as a non-dualistic state of being in which the mind of the person merges with Christ Consciousness.

What does this mean? We are enlightened and living a spiritually cool life. Yes, girlfriends it is time to spread our angel wings and fly to the heavens because the dinner parties will reveal our true spiritual nature. In time, we come to know that we have already awakened and there is no need to seek so hard. We simply reclaim what already is within us and learn to shine. Each dining event will provide the faith needed to honor and embrace this intuitively based insight.

Music

Music is another ritual to be added to the parties. Sacred ballads tend to be heard at most religious and spiritual gatherings. Major research data is available to prove that music has a healing vibration with every note played. Yes, an energy that can actually heal the body, mind and soul. A suggested list of known artists and compositions will be offered. The music will match the healing frequency of each party. The song arrangements for each soiree will strongly affect the outcome of the evening.

Color

Color is a restorative theme and healing vibration. Let the colors be apparent and boldly stand out for each gathering. Identify shades that feel good and ones that are not favorites. One hue is listed for each party, but feel free to add as much color to the gala as you want. Fearlessly paint the celebration and table setting with brilliant color.

Dress up for each party and feel the excitement grow. The perfect outfit will depend upon a conscious willingness. What piece of clothing fits your mood and the party theme? Suggestions have been made for each gathering. The intention is to unleash the creative energy within. Play dress up and fearlessly step into the closet. If your clothes feel lifeless, call a girlfriend and go through her favorite items—share the fun. If you are used to being safe with your clothes then try outlandish. Elegant is fine but find a new classy with a twist. If sloppy but chic is your uniform, shake it up. Leave your comfort zone. Make some bold changes and internalize a sense of empowerment. True liberation is a new approach to dressing and fabulous shoes. It is time to embrace a unique colorful self.

Essential oils

Most of us will have limited knowledge on how to use essential oils. Do we use a drop or two on our heads, bottom of the feet or behind the ears? Even women who enjoy oils and have a working knowledge may not be savvy enough to identify a high-quality, pure oil from one that has been diluted. The application in this instance is to become aware of superior oils and share this information with girlfriends. The dinner parties encourage the hostess to introduce therapeutic high-grade pure oils into the menu. Do the research and teach the other girls what has been discovered. Do use the oils with **caution** and only a few drops at a time.

Young Living oils are mentioned in this book. This company produces high-quality healing products and can be found on the Internet and at www.jylauxter.com. It is healthful to add therapeutic-grade essential oils to the kitchen shelf as a new type of spice and healing herb.

Closing

The ritual for closing a sacred event can be just as important as opening a spiritual evening. The details for next month's get-together will need to be discussed with the group members. Make sure every woman leaves happy and excited about the upcoming performance. Chat a little about the impending party to create a flurry of interest.

Then hug and kiss. Parties should be kept under three hours. It is important to consider family members who are waiting patiently at home for your return.

After party ritual

The dining affairs can heighten energies and for certain girlies there will need to be some down time to clear the liveliness. Most of us will have to be conscious and ground back into a safe place within ourselves. The word *ground* in this case means to be present in the moment, and this can be achieved by simply taking deep breaths below the naval center. Learn to breathe deeply and pull the earth into the body and exhale harmful emotions and pain. A peaceful and calm presence will soon follow. Each party will suggest effective ways to end a perfect night.

Conscious fortune cookie

The conscious fortune cookie is a final thought for the party, much like a Chinese fortune cookie prediction. Allow this metaphysical philosophy to penetrate on a deep level and be receptive to creating a new belief.

THE FIRST PARTY: SURVIVAL KIT

Overview

The first party teaches us to be conscious in the moment and rooted into the earth. Learn what it means to be anchored back into the physical realm and why this concept is so important for spiritual wellbeing. Sober up from past spiritual highs and feel the soil between the toes. We are spirits who have taken on bodies with an intention to have a comfortable, balanced earthly experience. Sometimes we forget and take our physical presence for granted. This party will create a solid foundation from which to grow.

Meat, potatoes and rooted vegetables should be served at this dinner, along with other sustainable favorites like eggs, beans, peas and tofu. These are foods that feed a strong earthy connection. Heat up the grill and offer a delicious skewered marinade of hormone-free meats and organic vegetables. Start the meal off with the healing powers of a freshly squeezed organic juice of beetroot, apple, carrot, celery and ginger, followed by a perky little pea pancake dripped with olive oil and freshly chopped heirloom tomatoes.

Learn what it means to be present in the moment as dinner is served on the floor, picnic style. Eat with the hands. Open the hips joints and feel the legs by securing the tailbone into the ground. Wrap comfy pillows with beautiful red printed fabric or invest in some red meditation cushions. This party might be one to take outdoors where the guests can feel alive and enjoy the elements of nature.

Sample Menu

A Chilled Goblet of Fresh-Squeezed Beet Juice

English Sweet Pea Pancakes topped with chopped Tomatoes & Parsley

Grilled Marinated Hormone-Free Beef
Skewered with Green & Red Bell Peppers,
Mushroom, Shallots & Cherry Tomatoes
Organic Micro-Greens sprinkled with Wolfberry Vinaigrette
Baked Scalloped Potatoes with Coconut Milk

Petite Red Beet Cupcakes & Wolfberry Cheesecake
Sun Kissed Organic Strawberries

Espresso

Recipe for Scalloped Potatoes with Coconut Milk

Ingredients

2 large onions
2 pounds (1 kilogram) potatoes
2 tablespoons coconut oil

2 tablespoons of fresh ginger
½ cup butter
4 garlic cloves, minced
tablespoon curry powder
1 1/2 cups coconut milk (one can)
1 tablespoon of rice wine
1 tablespoon of maple syrup
A bunch of fresh basil
Salt and freshly ground pepper to taste

Preparation

Preheat oven to 400 degrees Fahrenheit (200 degrees Celsius). Peel and slice potatoes into thin rounds. If possible, use a food processor. Put potatoes in a bowl of salted cold water. Set aside. Peel and slice onions into rounds. Heat oil and butter in a frying pan. Sauté the onions, garlic and ginger.

Add curry powder, wine, maple syrup and stir in coconut milk. Bring to a simmer. Add salt and pepper. Remove from heat. Drain potatoes.

In a greased 9-inch baking pan place half of the onion mixture. Cover with half of the potatoes. Layer with the rest of the onions and top with the rest of the potatoes. Pour the coconut milk mixture over the top. Bake, uncovered, at 400 degrees Fahrenheit (200 degrees Celsius) for 1 1/2 hours, or until a knife easily cuts through the layers of potatoes and the top of the dish is nicely browned. Garnish with fresh basil leaves. Serves 9.

Conscious life lesson

The life lesson is on a primal level as prayers go out to Mother Earth and family issues are healed. Learn to feel safe in the body and ask for help with challenging issues. Have the group individually share some life distractions—any issue that keeps a woman from moving forward on a trusted spiritual journey and feeling like she belongs here on earth. Share religious beliefs (God celebrated from traditional dogmas) and spiritual beliefs (God celebrated from an inner, personal intuitive space). Discuss what rituals insure a sane behavior when chaos hits. Have each gal convey her thoughts on how to develop a loving and conscious community. Go around the picnic blanket and speak to the meaning of consciousness. What does this word mean and personally represent? Openly relate any spiritual or religious practices that speak to living consciously.

Strengths

The higher aspects offered by this particular dinner party are the abilities to be present in the moment with happy thoughts, emotionally joyful and having a sense of security. There is a comfortable understanding of a life purpose. The healthy woman is focused, grounded and approachable. She will truly honor being alive and offer out into the world a perception of calm, love, gratefulness and grace. This woman spends less time judging others and prefers staying neutral by sharing her love. She respects the family tribe who birthed her into this world and will successfully find her own path, even under unhealthy circumstances. This girlfriend shows compassion to all souls.

Weaknesses

The lower aspect will replicate in a woman as a self-destructive trait. This characteristic presents itself as the following: extreme over or underweight, emotionally stressed, mean-spirited (unkind), frightened, fragile and spiritually unavailable. Perhaps a zany and unstable personality is apparent. There is also a strong disinterest in being consciously present. This girlfriend lives in survival mode and is quick to change her mind. She may even have suicidal tendencies. Unfortunately, there is an attachment to an obsessive personality with repeated destructive behaviors from the past. She will judge herself unfairly and always in a negative fashion. This friend will secretly be frustrated with someone—mother, father, ex-husband or children. The overachievers, rugged and ragged individuals with a *prove-it-to-me* attitude are simply the results of a strong lower aspect. Instead of running away from life, this woman may need to get grounded with some hugs and love from family, professionals and definitely her friends.

Go around the room and speak candidly on the strengths and weaknesses mentioned above. Share with the other girls any personal traits.

Healing ritual

After dinner, offer each girlfriend a footbath and foot massages. Have spa-like bath stations of warm water set up around the room. Sprinkle the baths with lavender sea salts and Jojoba oil. Add to the water herbs from the garden: fresh geranium, lavender, mint and lemongrass. Take turns offering foot massages or ask a favorite massage therapist to work the party. Lie back and relax with soothing music. After the foot ritual, take several deep inhales and exhales. Breathe all the way below the naval. With eyes closed, envision heaven and feel the earth. This is how it feels to be grounded and safe in the body.

Before meditation, continue to focus on deep breathing. Sit cross-legged on the floor with a straight spine and begin to take deep inhales and exhales through the noise. It will feel like the pelvis is literally moving forward and expanding with the inhale breath. On the exhale breath the body seems to rock backwards as the belly deflates. Inhale, hold and pull the chin into the chest and squeeze the base of the spine. On the exhale breath, relax the chin and pull the naval to the spine with a slight squeeze to the base of the tailbone. Try this breath work for 5-10 minutes.

Meditation

It is time to create a neutral space within the mind. Meditate on feeling safe and learn to trust the Divine order and shed needless worries. After meditation, discuss with the group how to calm daily fears. Use this time to discuss a personal life plan for creating a fearlessly alive and authentic woman.

Music

The perfect musical vibration for this party is in the note of C. Play Native American Indian music with the sound of drums. Let the music take on the beat of Mother Earth's heart. Listen to my favorite musician, named *Wah!* Her music speaks to the Earth Mother within. Invite a musician to entertain the group or offer drums to the girlfriends, then beat the night away! African music offers a remarkable resonance and is fitting for this party. Try some of the following performers: Mariza, Tinariwen, Maryann Mursal and Youssou N'Dour.

Color

Red will be the color of the evening. Look for the perfect shade to wear with black leggings, tall riding boots and a long flowing red silk shirt. If that doesn't match the mood, then try a pretty red cotton skirt with a fun short t-shirt that reads, *Save the Wales* or some other sustainable message. Buy a new or used pair of red cowboy boots then strut off to the party in a real forceful *yeehaw* way. Make sure to put on some bright red lipstick before entering the front door of the party.

Gather everything red—candles, table cloths, pillows and flowers. Use enough of the color to feel and see the results it has on the environment. Shades of red along with pink, cream and lavender can create an interesting appeal.

Essential oil

Frankincense is placed on the bottom of the feet after the footbath to ground the gals. This will offer a sense of security. Drops of frankincense oil can be used on the top of the head and behind the neck before meditating. Frankincense keeps out negative energies. Consider other oils for the party such as cedarwood, clove and vertiver. These oils are powerful and provide stable and grounding properties.

Closing

Chant the Adi Mantra three times for protection and a Divine connection:

Ong Namo Guru Dev (dave) Namo
I bow to the creative consciousness, I bow
to the teacher of Divine wisdom.

Remember to assign the next hostess, date (within a month if possible), time and location for the upcoming dinner party. Make sure all the girls leave with this vital information.

After party ritual

Take a bath and add one tablespoon each of sea salt and apple cider vinegar to the water. This will help clear the other girlfriends' energies and psychic attachments from the body. Do this new routine after each conscious dinner. If not too exhausted, grab a journal and do some writing. What has been learned, and what life changes can be implemented?

Conscious fortune cookie says:

The deeper the roots, the higher the spiritual journey and the more enlightened a woman will become.

THE SECOND PARTY: PLAY AND PASSION

Overview

The second party will help cultivate passion and playfulness back into life. It is time to release the stress and bring back the girlish ways of belly laughing and sassy spirits. It is an occasion to unleash the party girl within and all the bottled-up creativity. Think orange, then decorate. Hang variation of orange fabrics and paper balls from the ceiling to create a unique dining experience. Use recycled glass bottles and fill them with Gerber daisies to add beauty to the dinner table.

Salmon cakes will jump-start this party. Warm pumpkin soup garnished with caramelized onions and edible organic mum petals, served with a variety of fresh organic greens will offer the perfect main course. Cook a kettle of wild rice and smile. It is time to enjoy the richness of hot chocolate pudding cake accompanied by a yummy homemade apricot sorbet, then dance.

Get into the closet and find the most outrageous outfit. Maybe it is a perfect timeless, vintage look. Go outside or up to the attic and find elements to bring into the sacred play area, creating a theatrical space for the evening. This is the opportunity to be fearless, wild and full of expression.

Sample Menu

Freshly Squeezed Carrot, Apple, Lemon with Ginger Juice
A slice of Orange to Garnish

Salmon Cakes with Homemade Garlic Mayonnaise & Fresh Dill

Pumpkin Soup topped with Caramelized Onions
Red Wild Rice
Organic Garden Herbs with Orange Dressing
Goat Cheese Popover & Pumpkin Bread Foie Gras Tea Sandwich

Warm Chocolate Pudding Cake
Apricot Sorbet

Sage & Tangerine Tea

Recipe for Chocolate Pudding Cake

Ingredients

1/3 cup unsweetened chocolate
½ cup melted unsalted butter
1 1/3 cups sucanat sugar
1 cup flour
1 ½ teaspoons baking powder
½ teaspoon sea salt
½ cup milk

½ cup dark brown sugar
3 tablespoons unsweetened coca
2 teaspoons vanilla
2 tablespoons rum
1 ½ cups boiling water

Preparation

Preheat oven to 350 degrees Fahrenheit (175 degrees Celsius).

Grease a 9-inch square pan.

In a double boiler, melt chocolate.

Combine butter and half of the sucanat sugar then add flour, baking powder, sea salt and milk.

Fold melted chocolate into mixture and pour into pan.

In a separate bowl, stir together remaining sugar, brown sugar and cocoa. Sprinkle over the batter in pan. Bring water to a boil and add vanilla & rum. Pour water slowly over batter and bake for an hour. Serve hot and straight from the oven.

Serves 9.

Conscious life lesson

Find the sacredness in passion and learn how to create and play again without the emotional adult hang-ups. Healing is on an energetic lusty front by allowing the true party girl to emerge without guilt. Confide a secret passion to the girlfriends. Describe some magical ways to express a zest for living. Stay within the context of the theme with healthy feelings exchanged. Talk willingly with the girls about creating something from nothing and how to expand the character of one's self.

Note for teenage girls: Use this party to discuss the sacredness of sexuality and the important issues surrounding womanhood.

Strengths

With this dining affair, higher aspects manifest in a woman's life by becoming the following: creationist (one who freely expresses), visionary, pioneer, healer, master of many trades, warrior, fierce lover and an inventor. These strengths can help a woman create harmony for herself and in the lives of others. This gal is the mystic, and she is able to see another person's higher aspects. Strong intuitive gifts will be this woman's life blessings. The higher aspect reveals itself as a powerful and pure energy source. This girlfriend will be able to harness this raw creative force and focus her attention on self-expression. Rejuvenation is the message she offers to others. Expect this woman to be a natural healer who is sweet natured with great popularity among her friends. Freedom and creative expression is of utmost importance in her life. A positive life path will probably favor that of an artist or healer.

Weaknesses

Lower aspects will be represented in the following ways: a self-destructive tendency, loss of identity, playing the victim role and stressing. This woman allows chaos and drama into her life. There tend to be abusive habits, self-loathing and passive-aggressive behaviors. Abundance in every area of life is very hard to manifest when this weakness is strong. This girlfriend may become depressed, consumed with lusty thoughts or lose focus. She may also show signs of sexual addictions and strong emotions around money and power. The constant desire to fix people, to the point of smothering friends or family members, is a sign of weakness. This woman may also seek perfectionism to a fault with a strong undertow of unworthiness. Be a loving pal, for this girlfriend needs a hand to hold.

Go around the room and speak candidly on the strengths and weaknesses mentioned above. Share with the other girls any personal traits.

Healing ritual

Invite a yoga teacher or Tai Chi master to teach a class before dinner. Another idea is to form a sacred circle and dance. Use orange scarves to wave into the air as an expression of freedom and move all troubles and fears away. Afterward create a group ritual to heal the victim within. Use the powerful energy of the other women to manifest creative ways to safely connect with inner passions.

Before meditation, sit cross-legged with a tall spine and begin to focus on deep breathing. Inhale through the nose all the way below the navel. Fill the belly with the breath and exhale, pulling the navel center into the spine. Continue to take deep inhales and exhales. Now place the hands around the ankles. On the inhale breath, pull the chest up and roll back the shoulders. Exhale the naval center into the spine, allowing the shoulder to slightly roll forward. Keep the head straight and avoid bobbing with the movement. This is called spinal flex. Continue with the spinal exercise for 3-5 minutes.

Meditation

With eyes closed, place attention on the womb. Send love and light to the pelvis. Honor the sacredness and grace of being a woman. Go around the sacred circle and discuss the outcome from the meditation. If the womb had a voice, what would it say?

Music

The healing vibration for this party is music set in the note of D. Bring out the favorite upbeat tunes and dance away. Michael Bublé has a great voice and his music makes the feet want to move. Find the right songs to celebrate the night. Other favorite musicians are Sting, Jamie Collins, Ali Milner, Emmanauel Jai, Shikisha and Mikey Wax.

Color

Celebrate the color orange for this party. Girlfriends get creative and express this color in the right look. Throw on a pair of comfy, old worn-out jeans, a pair of fun boots, add a funky scarf and a bright orange cashmere sweater or go for the totally opposite look with a pretty, princess party dress in shades of oranges. Think *sassy girl* and put on a short skirt, fishnet stockings and high heels. Is there nothing orange in the wardrobe? It must be time to go shopping and buy a new pair of bright orange slim cut straight-legged jeans or a comfy, slouchy but flattering pair of dark orange or coral trousers. Throw on a pair on ballerina flats and spring off to the party. Find your own look and celebrate this creative flair.

Essential oil

Tangerine, ylang ylang and sandalwood are the oils for the evening. Sandalwood is powerful for skin problems and wrinkles. For a youthful glow, place a couple drops in a facial night cream and kiss wrinkles and blemishes goodnight. Add 1-2 drops of tangerine oil to the dessert or water glasses. Garnish with a fresh slice of orange.

Closing

Finish the evening with an original protective prayer. As a group, design and voice a passionate prayer. The hostess might want to say a couple of uplifting jingles to bless this second dinner party.

After party ritual

In private, contemplate then write about personal resentments or fears toward the lusty, party girl within. Take a moment to acknowledge *forgiveness.* Say a prayer and ask the angels to remove any shame.

Conscious fortune cookie says:

A life of expressed passions will lead to a magical journey with many opportunities and intuitive gifts.

THE THIRD PARTY: POWER AND TRUTH

Overview

The third party focuses on the seriousness of owning personal power and honesty. This party probably won't feel as light and airy as the previous one. Don't let the P-O-W-E-R word cause trepidation. Think about how the sun shines upon the earth. Be a glowing gal with an overflowing persuasive essence for all to see. Let the world, family and friends see an inner almighty strength and at the same time, a unique sunny presence.

Start the meal with a delicious detoxing celery and fennel soup made with a dash of truth and served with a Japanese green tea matcha muffin, hot from the oven. Grilled cod fillets splashed with fresh lemon, scallions and ghee is the main dish. Biryani, a Persian favorite, will accompany the fish and is served with garden vegetables topped with bouquets of fresh mint and coriander. End the meal on a sweet note by serving homemade banana bread with chocolate chunks and a lemon granadilla tart.

The Power and Truth party will lead the group to discuss techniques for owning personal power. This party is a bit more staid and perfect for a formal dining experience. Bring out the good China and yellow lace tablecloths with matching napkins, then light the candelabras.

Sample Menu

*Freshly Squeezed Pineapple, a splash of
Lemon, Lavender & Mint Garnish*

Celery & Fennel Soup served with Matcha Muffins

*Vegetable Biryani topped with Coriander & Mint Leaves
Grilled Cod Fillets
A side of Lemon Yogurt Sauce*

Lemon Granadilla Tart & Chocolate Banana Bread

Chai Indian Tea

Recipe for Vegetable Biryani

Ingredients

*2 cups basmati rice
4 cups water
2 tablespoons of ghee
4 tablespoons of oil
1 cup sliced onions
1 tablespoon chopped green chili
1 teaspoon ginger
1 teaspoon garlic*

1/2 teaspoon chili powder
1/2 teaspoon turmeric powder
2 teaspoons garam masala
3 cups vegetables: Tomato, corn, carrot, cauliflower, green peas, squash
½ cup of yogurt
¼ cup of cashew nuts
Salt to taste
¼ cup of coriander and mint leaves

Preparation

Rinse rice then cook with ½ teaspoon of salt and ghee. Set aside.

Heat oil in a large saucepan and sauté onions until golden, add ginger, garlic & green chili. Add chili powder, turmeric powder and garam masala, then add vegetables, yogurt and nuts. Cover and simmer until vegetables are cooked.

Combine the above vegetable curry with rice. Serves 9.

Conscious life lesson

The third party teaches a woman to own her truth and power in a time when the world is still dominated by male aggressive energy. For example, in some cultures in the Middle East women are forbidden to show their power or even their faces. It is a God-given right for all females to have personal power and voices that can be heard.

People around the planet lead with the strong yang element and may not appreciate the presence of a powerful, yet meek, yin essence. A truly powerful gal uses both an active feminine energy and a solid masculine force. This means girlfriends have both polarities within themselves. This is an important life lesson. Women who are steady and live a balanced, happy life will understand how to merge softness into a powerful, firm presence.

Discuss among the group of friends, what it means to own personal power in a balanced way. What does it mean to be a woman who is unique, soft and feminine, yet powerful? Check to see if power still represents the *clawing your way* to the top mentality learned in a male dominated sociality. It is time to add a whimsical spiritual foundation to the list of powerful traits to ensure a commanding life full of integrity.

Strengths

This dinner party helps a woman understand the higher aspects of a charismatic leader, truth giver and a person of authority. She represents authenticity and is a true skeptic. This power gal allows her true strengths to be revealed without cowering. By understanding and believing in herself, she is able to stay strong and see the truth. This truth transcends all religious and dogmatic attempts to frame it. She makes a huge impact on others as she seeks fairness at all cost. Her strength represents a strong spiritual leadership quality and a woman who is not afraid of escorting the world forward into brighter days. She will believe that true wealth is the ability to control greed and materialism. It is this woman's nature to act as the protector of innocent souls, and she has the ability to nurture the world. As a born leader, her path will transmute negative energy into a positive light. She will no doubt make a strong contribution to new forms of sociality.

Weaknesses

The lower aspect for this woman results in constant power struggles with others. She tends to be frightened to believe in her personal strengths, even though she might come off as a bit arrogant. There is a strong ego presence because of a serious lack of confidence. Narcissism can be a major part of this gal's distinctive character. A noticeable weakness is a manipulative behavior that she uses to control her friends. This girlfriend harbors anger and can take things personally. Procrastination over decisions can lead to major problems in life. It seems when this weakness is strong there will be fear and pain around making the right decision. Greed is a major obstacle in this woman's life and her personal agenda is, "What's in it for me and how can I make this situation worth my while?" She may be the type of girlfriend who is up for a vicious vengeance and at times socially irresponsible. This woman from time to time needs to insulate herself from others and dreads exclusion and public humiliation. Looking good and making it to the top at the cost of others may start to become a life mantra. Desiring power for the sake of being the most powerful, plus her inflexible, dogmatic positions, will have some karmic consequences. It may be time to keep this girlfriend honest with healthy and gentle communications.

Go around the room and speak candidly on the strengths and weaknesses mentioned above. Share with the other girls any personal traits.

Healing ritual

Form a sacred circle and have the group come to a standing position. Begin to twist from the waist, keeping the feet flat on the ground and allow the head and shoulder to flow gently with the movement. Feel and honor the belly. Continue to move the midsection of the body with some powerful music, then allow the legs and arms to join in on the fun. When the movement has settled, have the ladies come back to a neutral cross-legged seated position.

Try a breathing technique called breath of fire. During this breath, the naval center is quickly pulled into the spine on the exhale breath, immediately followed by a short quick inhale as the naval is released. Repeat, and remember to breathe only through the nose. This breath is done very quickly with a pulsing action above the naval.

Go around the circle and share ideas on what it means to be powerful. Let others empower the person sharing by clapping hands, yelling praise or simply sounding the bells. Give this woman the praise she deserves. It is time to build group confidence.

Arts and crafts: Design crowns made for a queen by constructing a new age conscious headdress. Begin this process by gluing brightly colored yellow feathers, bold fabric or lace on an inexpensive plastic headband. If made in advance, use to decorate the dinner table. Another suggestion is to buy, borrow or rent tiaras and wear them throughout the night to symbolize royal power.

Meditation

Have the group close their eyes and ask for a powerful spiritual force to join in the meditative state. Communicate with a powerful higher self or spirit guide. The strength that comes from the spirit realm is the same feeling of the powerful woman who lives within. Exchange with your girlfriends the power you feel while accessing this intense spiritual force.

Music

The musical note of E is the vibration for this party. Pick commanding and soulful music for the evening. Listen to compositions from the following artists: Chris Botti, Colin Bullock, Josh Groban and Indigo Girls.

Color

Brighten up the night and add some power with the color, yellow and shine. If yellow is just not your color—think champagne or a light tan. How can a powerful message be expressed in the clothing worn? What does it mean to dress powerfully? Does power still represent a man's black business suit? If yes is the answer to that question, then it is definitely time to go shopping for something fabulous, feminine and powerful—not sexy, that was last's month party. Smile.

Essential oil

Effective oils that can be added into the home and definitely for the dinner party are: lemon, bergamot, lavender and rosemary. Lemon and lavender can be used in cooking. Try making the lemon granadilla tart with real essential oils and taste the difference. Definitely use a couple drops of lavender and lemon oils in the homemade pineapple cocktail. Clean up after the party using lemon oil on the dishtowel or in the dishwater. Notice the difference in the way the kitchen smells when the duties have been finished.

Closing

Gather in a circle and chant OM three times. Then read a powerful quote from a favored historical woman leader. There is nothing better than contributing an influential woman mentor to your girlfriends.

After party ritual

Arrive home and sip some herbal tea and write three powerful statements about yourself, then tape the list to a mirror. For the next three days admire the list and feel empowered.

Conscious fortune cookie says:

A woman who is not afraid of being spiritually powerful will help many people in her lifetime.

THE FOURTH PARTY: LOVE FEAST

Overview

The fourth party will align the group's energy to giving and receiving love. All the parties are endearing, but this gathering might bring up some extra emotions as hearts shift and intimacy grows. Don't be afraid to be vulnerable and speak from a sweet space within. Shed a few tears and let love into the evening. Dim the lights and gather up pink and green candles (10-15) to create a cozy atmosphere.

The vibration from green and pink will reflect the power of love. Decide what to wear and how to set the table by embracing both of these perky shades. Bring heart-felt love energy into the party and pink rose petals onto the table. Place green boxes on the dinner plates with a heart surprise waiting inside. Give the gift of unconditional love and let this feeling be felt throughout the evening.

A wonderful menu idea for this party is to serve roasted chicken garnished with a rose sauce. This is an opportunity to cook with a therapeutic-grade essential oil of rose. Make sure you have some organic rose petals on hand in the kitchen to use in this fabulous dish. Expect girlfriends to fall in love as they sip their green healing cocktails made with freshly juiced spinach, apples, celery, lemon, parsley and cucumber. If watermelon is in season, juice one whole melon and pinch your lips. Feel the love grow with tarragon asparagus spears sautéed in ghee and kissed with honey.

Contemplate making nondairy homemade ice cream to escort a hot peach cobbler. It is so easy and much healthier than most store bought. Start by putting 2 ½ cups of raw cashews and water from 2 young coconuts into a blender and mix until smooth. Add 2 cups of agave nectar, ½ cup Bariani olive oil and 4 cups of organic strawberries and blend again until creamy. Pour the mixture into an ice cream maker and voilà

Sample Menu

Garden Green Juice garnished with Slices of Cucumber

Heart-Shaped Spinach Ravioli with Sage & Burnt Butter

Roasted Rose Chicken
Tarragon Honey Asparagus Spears
Fresh Water Cress

Warm Old-Fashioned Peach Cobbler
Homemade Cashew Ice Cream

Chamomile Tea

Recipe for Rose Chicken

Ingredients

5-9 pound Roasting Chicken
4 garlic cloves, crushed
½ cup of chicken stock or white wine
1 teaspoon of salt & pepper
1 tablespoon of ghee

Preparation

Cook chicken for approximately 20 minutes per pound at 350 degrees Fahrenheit (175 degrees Celsius). Start by washing the chicken with water to clear any bacteria. Take out the giblets. Rub ghee and garlic over the skin. Salt and pepper the outside and inside of the bird. Roast the chicken in the oven and baste with stock or white wine.

Sauce

10-15 organic rose petals
5-10 organic dry hazelnuts
1 tablespoon of ghee
4-7 drops of rose oil
2 cloves of garlic
1 tablespoon of maple syrup
2 cups of white wine
½ cup of goji berry juice

In a food processor, grind the nuts and rose petals. In a large saucepan heat the ghee and begin adding garlic and nuts/petals. Slowly add the wine, maple syrup and juice. Let simmer and reduce for about 30 minutes. Thinly slice the chicken and serve with sauce. Right before serving add the rose oil, either directly to each dish (1-2 drops) or to the sauce (4-7 drops). Serves 9 people.

Conscious life lesson

Love is a strong vibration and can be an extra hard lesson to review. For some gals, major love blocks shield their chest, keeping them from experiencing deep loving relationships. How can protective hearts to be opened to the magic of love? Discuss loving another person and self-love. Offer personal tips to self-care when major fear swells up around being lovable. In a sacred circle, set the past free by sharing with girlfriends how to recover from past heartaches or wounded childhoods.

Strengths

The love dinner party teaches women to open their hearts and share their souls. A healthy and balanced girlfriend can be an anchor for her peers. She is an innate healer and a person who is available to deeply care for many different types of people at the same time. This woman is not afraid to be heart centered. She can admit feelings of purity and is grateful for a life of grace. Her ability to love others and have healthy boundaries will inspire her friends. This woman is empathetic and wouldn't think of sabotaging her life with unresolved emotional feelings or a chaotic lifestyle. She understands that her calm nurturing presence (no ego) can heal a person. In fact, on an unconscious level, people will seek her energy for healing. Confused sometimes by her own professional calling, she finds great pleasure helping others with their life purpose. This gal is truly empathetic and is a natural born healer regardless of whether she ever pursues a career in the healthcare field.

Weaknesses

Weak emotional boundaries with friends and family will create an imbalance to this girlfriend's character. When this weakness is strong she feels naïve. There is a sense of not being able to turn off feelings. In some cases, this highly sensitive woman might be in a room full of people absorbing the negative, chaotic energy and all of a sudden become claustrophobic with a strong urge to run away. This gal is very empathetic. When she is emotionally stressed, it is hard for her to think straight and there can be a loss of identity. Be aware that this is a sign that the lower aspect has taken over. She has become an emotional pincushion and is ungrounded. "I am not worthy of love," becomes her mantra and shows up in an unattractive, needy way. Pride is a big weakness for this woman. It is time for loving girlfriends to step in and rescue by reflecting back her God-given strengths.

Go around the room and speak candidly on the strengths and weaknesses mentioned above. Share with the other girls any personal traits.

Healing ritual

Invite a spiritual healer who can offer a commanding *love* presentation. Speak to emotional fatigue and anxiety when the heart vitality is depleted. Have the speaker address transmuting negative energies and suggest ways for developing healthy boundaries with effective methods for clearing personal space. Sit back, listen, learn and receive. Check in with the girlfriends because there might be a teacher or spiritual healer among the group of friends who would invite the opportunity to speak on this topic.

Before meditation, focus on deep inhales and exhales. After the breathing exercise, take the index and middle figure and tap lightly on the thymus gland located at the collarbone. This action has a magical way of resetting the heart energy.

Meditation

Place the hands on the chest. Connect with the heart and send love by shining an imaginary pink light straight to the upper body. Think about the people in your life who have inflicted pain. Fire up the love juices and send love to all of them. There is an abundance of love to be absorbed from the universe during this earthly experience. Set some ambitious love goals for accessing, absorbing and sending more love energy, then share ideas with the group.

Music

The musical note of F is the vibration for this party. Classical music offers a higher vibration of love. Also test new age artist, Deva Premal and partner, Miten. Pick tunes that will inspire love. Jack Johnson and the French singer, Lara Fabian are favored by many.

Color

Pink and green are the colors for the evening. Go with both or just one and let the heart energy into the gala event. A pink shawl or silk scarf to wrap in is a beautiful soft touch. A high-spirited green dress with pink tights and a pair of jazzy short boots could be a great look. Don't forget to wear a pink quartz gemstones necklace and lots of springy bangles.

Arts and crafts: Take cardboard and cut out heart shapes. Paint, draw or glue objects found in nature on the hearts enlivening an inner love essence. Cut a hole at the top and pull pink grosgrain ribbon through the hearts and create a *love support* necklace.

Essential oil

Rose, marjoram and yarrow are the primary oils for this affair. Rose has an extremely high vibration and when placed on the heart shows great healing power. Don't forget to use rose oil in the chicken dish. It truly makes such a difference.

Closing

On a piece of paper have the girls write down one or several undesirable character traits. These are unattractive mannerisms that belong to themselves or ones they see in others that they do not like. By identifying unwanted behaviors, it becomes easier to identify naughty girlfriends and when it is time to set clear boundaries with them. Sit in a circle. Each girl will speak out loud her unacceptable personas. Send around a large, nonflammable bowl and set the piece of paper on fire. Each girl will drop the burning paper inside the bowl then say a silent prayer. Please be **cautious** and keep the fire in the container.

Release and let go. Learn to be respectfully in the moment and create a safe circle for everyone to feel loved. It is time to become responsible by setting clear boundaries. Rebirth and give yourself permission to set clear limitations with girlfriends.

Keep in mind that boundaries are not actions of retaliation. Make sure to understand the difference. Boundaries are a form of guidelines, rules or limits that a person creates for safety. Retaliation, on the other hand, is a force of pay-back energy and reflects damage based on feeling overpowered. Many times a girlfriend will say she is creating healthy boundaries, when, on the contrary, she is simply lashing out. This is an example of a woman who unconsciously wants her friend to feel her pain. If there is time, this important topic may need to be further discussed.

After party ritual

In bed and right before going to sleep, inhale and lift the left hand to the mouth and kiss the figure tips. Exhale, hand down. Inhale, lift the right hand to the lips and kiss the figure tips. Exhale, hand down. Continue back and forth until sleep overcomes the body.

Conscious fortune cookie says:

A woman who allows herself true love, discovers her spirit and will live a meaningful and long life.

The Fifth Party: Heaven on Earth

Overview

The fifth party represents grounding communications and freely accepting our psychic abilities. This dinner teaches a woman to be an ambassador for the spirit realm. Celebrate the color blue and decorate the dining room appropriately with bright hues of blues: napkins, tablecloths and name cards. This is the night to sing, chant and verbalize spiritual truths to the girlfriends. Before dinner, have all the gals stand around the dining table and sing a blessing for the healing foods and sacred sisterhood. Shift the energy in the room by simply singing then take a moment of silence to feel the difference.

Start the evening with a cooling homemade ginger ale perfect for digestion and preparing the throat for conversation. Spunky vegetarian nori rolls with a garnish of fresh bean sprouts are the appetizer du jour and a nutritious way to kick off the fifth dinner. Soba noodles and sear Bluefin tuna served on a bed of arugula will be the suggested main menu choice and a pure delight for the guests. Offer a beautiful tray of mini sponge cakes topped with fresh blueberries and agave syrup for dessert. Get in the kitchen and whip up something extraordinary. How about a chocolate mousse recipe that calls for avocado and raw cacao—a chocolate mousse that is so delicious and healthy?

Let this party teach the power of communication and watch your manners—speak not with a mouth full of food. It is time to use a strong voice and be heard. Consider this to be a *Guru Girlfriend* coming-out party.

Sample Menu

*Homemade Ginger Ale blended with a Splash of Grape Juice
Garnish with Seedless Grapes*

Vegetable Nori Roll-Ups

*Asian Soba Noodles topped with Sear Bluefin Tuna and Arugula
Endive & Steamed Broccoli Florets to garnish*

Blueberry Agave Sponge Cake & Raw Chocolate Avocado Mousse

Japanese Matcha Green Tea

Recipe for Asian Noodles

Ingredients

*1 8-ounce package buckwheat soba noodles
¼ cup of toasted sesame seeds
¼ cup chopped cilantro
½ cup chopped scallions
¼ cup chopped red cabbage*

Sauce

> *3 tablespoons of toasted sesame oil*
> *4 tablespoons tamari or soy sauce*
> *4 tablespoons balsamic vinegar*
> *1 tablespoon maple syrup*
> *1 tablespoon hot pepper oil*

Preparation

Cook soba noodles and cool. Add to the noodles the seeds, cilantro, scallions and red cabbage. Combine sauce ingredients above and pour over noodles and toss.

Conscious life lesson

Learn to channel spiritual truths and become the educator. Heal the energy in the throat by voicing the teacher within. It is time to live at a higher frequency. Take a moment to share with each other what it means to consciously communicate. Learn to have faith in a Divine presence. Articulate what cannot be said by bringing a higher level of consciousness down to the earth plane with every spoken word. If 90% of all communications is energy then how well are you communicating?

Strengths

Living in the higher aspect means being the step-down transformer for God and a trusted communicator. This woman is the teacher and an inspiration. She has the courage to stand up and share a spiritual message. She is an ambassador for a higher purpose and networks with others to get favorable results. The gal who is the teacher will be an anchor and channel for heaven on this earth plane. This saintly soul represents what it means to feel good in the body and live a spiritually cool life. The gift this woman shares is that she can openly articulate a spiritual message that others clamor to understand. She is the destroyer of illusions and offers a higher vibration to her soul-group. This is a strong intuitive and telepathic person who heals others with the sound of her voice. Encourage this girlfriend to become a popular teacher.

Weaknesses

The lower aspect of character appears when this woman acts a bit aloof or detached. She may often feel alone, overlooked and misunderstood by the world. These are signs of not being grounded and not conscious in the moment. Unfortunately, this girlfriend can be a bit of a *know-it-all* and if not careful, she can hurt others with her careless words. When this gal goes missing, she has become a hermit and this is a clear sign for change and healing. Excessive talking is an unbalanced trait and clearly a weakness. This woman can get caught up in becoming the mentalist. She is unable to transcend the active thinking mind and in the end will miss becoming the channel for a higher dimension. Feelings of spiritlessness, emptiness and pessimism are qualities of this woman when she lives in her lower aspect and surely a good time to bring in the girlfriends.

Go around the room and speak candidly on the strengths and weaknesses mentioned above. Share with the other girls any personal traits.

Healing ritual

Pick a favorite song, chant or quote from a famous master like Buddha and sing it until the vibration of the words can be felt. Invite a musician to dinner and sing along. Chant and create a healing circle. Gather the girls, sit side by side and hold hands. The left hand is used to receive love and healing, (palm up) and the right hand is used to give love, (palm down). Begin chanting Ra, Ma, Da, Sa, Sa, Say, So, Hung. This ancient healing chant can be found on the CD called, *Grace* by Snatam Kaur.

Before meditation, gently do some neck rolls. Inhale, and on the exhale breath drop the left ear to the left shoulder. Inhale back to center, then exhale the right ear to the right shoulder. Repeat several times. Breathe and rotate the head in a clockwise motion. Continue the head rotations for several repetitions, then reverse the movement.

Meditation

Meditate on becoming a channel for a higher realm. After five minutes of silence, share with girlfriends ideas for effective ways to spiritually communicate with friends and family. It is time to manifest the teacher within. Visualize a tree and its powerful roots, then become the vision. From a grounded place, live and speak many truths. Focus on the throat during meditation. The party might take on a more magical tone by girlfriends opening up to speak their truths. There may be a need for extra time for the women to express unresolved issues left over from the past.

Music

The musical note of G is the vibration for this party. Listen to singer, songwriter and yogi, Snatam Kaur with Guru Ganesha. Perhaps listen to John Mayer. His lyrics provide many insights to living and loving.

Color

Blue is the color for the fifth party. Balance the blue throughout the house and on the dinner table with other bright colors. Use this hue to access the energy for robust communications. Think Guru and dress as if you just stepped off the plane back from a tour of India. A bright blue tunic over a favorite pair of pants or leggings might be the perfect look, or how about a swing dress printed with bold blue flowers? Have a pair of shoes in your closet that make a real statement and haven't been worn in a while? Tonight is the night to slip on those Cinderella slippers and party. Pick an outfit that creates confidence, then speak some truths.

Essential oil

Eucalyptus, sage and frankincense are the oils to be used for this party. Place 10 drops each of these three oils in a medium-size spray bottle with fresh water then mist the throat. Completely shift the energies in the room by spraying the oil into the air.

Closing

Close the evening with a personal name invocation. Each girl will say the following phrase: "I (birth name) am a precious child of God." When everyone has finished saying the prayer, ring the Tibetan bells three times.

After party ritual

Write a list of ways to stay grounded and conscious as you speak spiritual truths. Then practice these techniques daily for 40 days.

Conscious fortune cookie says:

A woman who experiences big life lessons needs to teach what she has learned and all is coming.

THE SIXTH PARTY: INTUITION

Overview

The color purple will heal and offer support as the intuitive transformations activate. Bring out the fairies, angels and spirit guides, because this is going to be a magical evening. Discover what voices within are of true guidance. Understand why it is critical to have a meditation practice.

Serve a light meal for healing. Take the forks away and offer chopsticks that will later serve as magic wands. Try a fresh spring roll smothered with homemade peanut sauce served on a bed of seaweed salad. Continue healing the body with an organic kale dish. Save room for an Acai smoothie bowl for dessert. This super food will provide extra energy as the group connects with spiritual highs and beyond.

Clear the day and the palate with a cooling Ayurveda purification potion. Blend together: four pitted dates, ten sprouted almonds, two frozen bananas, one cup of coconut milk and one cup of organic soy or rice milk. Pour mixture into frozen martini glasses, sprinkle with freshly ground cardamom and cinnamon. Garnish with a fussy cocktail umbrella.

Sample Menu

Purification Potion

Fresh Purple Cabbage Spring Rolls on a bed of Seaweed Salad
With Homemade Peanut Sauce

Raw Marinated Kale Salad
Homemade Flaxseed Crackers

Acai Bowl Topped with Chunks of Chocolate,
Chopped Nuts and Coconut Flakes
Fresh Mint Tea

Raw Marinated Kale Salad

Ingredients

2 cups of shiitake mushrooms
8 cups of shredded kale
½ cup hijiki seaweed (presoak for 2 hours, drain)
3 cups of carrots
3 cups of cucumbers
1 cup sesame seeds

Garnish with 3 cups teriyaki almonds
2½ cups almonds soaked for 12 hours in purified water
1/3 cup chopped dates
¼ cup Nama Shoyu
2 garlic cloves
1 tablespoon minced fresh ginger

Marinade

½ cup lemon juice
½ cup Nama Shoyu

Preparation

Teriyaki almonds—combine the dates, Nama Shoyu, garlic and ginger in a food processor and grind until smooth. Coat the almond in the paste. Dehydrate at 145 degrees for an hour. Turn down the temperature to 115 degrees and continue to dehydrate.

In a large bowl combine the above ingredients and toss in marinade. Garnish with teriyaki almonds and create a large bowl with leaves of bib lettuce. Serve your 9 guests this healthy and delicious salad.

Conscious life lessons

Learn to honor gut feelings. The intuition can be very powerful and useful when life gets difficult. Contemplate the purpose of meditation or the neutral space and how it relates to retrieving intuitive powers. Discuss any personal meditation practices. Share with girlfriends any changes that have occurred since developing a devotional routine. Talk among the group and speak openly to the magic of meditation and specifically to intuitive powers and spiritual gifts.

Strengths

This woman is clairsentient. Clairsentience is the most prevalent psychic gift in our society today. This girlfriend knows that which cannot be known. She is the prophet and can manifest for the world what is so greatly needed by seeing it first in her mind's eye, then downloading to the rest of us. It is okay to be this gifted. She shares company with other girls who are not looking to steal energy or compete with her gifts. This gal can cherish her brilliant mind, yet can be gentle to her own spirit and heart. Self-control, wisdom and non-attachment are qualities when this woman is balanced and living from her higher aspect. She excels in self-inventing, self-discoveries and can easily embrace a contemplative lifestyle. This girlfriend receives great satisfaction from helping others in the world.

Weaknesses

The hardest task for this friend is to learn to be in her heart and not in her head. Unfortunately, when weaknesses creep into this gal's life, she tends to be confused, unavailable and consistently in her mind thinking about what to do next. The mantra of this weakness is "Why don't I get it and why do I struggle so deeply to understand my own existence?" Neurological and psychological disorders can appear if this woman doesn't maintain balance in her life. "I think I feel," are words often spoken by this girlfriend, instead of being sure of her true feelings. This gal will struggle with fatigue, confusion and tend to be a bit dazed and flaky at times. She may suffer from insomnia and headaches. Depression can also be a constant health threat to this girlfriend when she is unbalanced for too long. Attention friends, it is time to rally and help this soul sister integrate her powerful self so she can help the planet grow.

Go around the room and speak candidly on the strengths and weaknesses mentioned above. Share with the other girls any personal traits.

Healing ritual

Ask a psychic or intuitive healer to come and perform a group reading. Invite this professional to describe her own gifts and how the psychic abilities have been nurtured and blossomed. Arts and craft might be to have friends design spirit wands for themselves. This night might turn out to be a Harry Potter's night out for grown-ups, so make sure to bring in the floating candles.

Create a ritual where the wands are empowered by magic and use them to transform each woman onto the next level of sisterhood. In other words, create a formal ceremony for the little witch within— we are talking about a good, white spiritual witch, of course. Try to keep this rite organic and stay out of the Wiccan handbooks. Let the intuition run wild and be raw.

Before meditation, close the eyes and take deep inhales and exhales. Sit cross-legged with a tall straight spine. Take the index figure and thumb of both hands and make a connection. Allow the hands to sit on the lap or knees and with the breath begin mentally chanting Sa, Ta, Na, Ma (infinity, life, death, rebirth). The gaze is at the middle of the head. Imagine a violet-colored flame burning at the forehead. For more seasoned yoginis, chant: Gobinday, Mukanday, Udaray, Aparay, Hareeung, Kareeung, Niraamay, Akamay. This is a mantra for liberation.

Meditation

Meditate on the neutral space within and request guidance to access this powerful place. Ask the following question before closing the eyes, "If all the answers to life's questions and concerns are within me just waiting to be revealed and only accessible by stilling the mind, then why hasn't stilling the mind become a priority in my life? What is standing in the way of creating a new healthy habit?"

Discuss the fears around this practice and answer the question, "What is my excuse for not meditating on a regular basis?" Set some new rules for embracing meditation and share them with the girlfriends.

Music

The musical note of A is the vibration for this party. Bring out the true prophets of their days like: The Beatles, John Lennon, Cats Stevens (Yusuf) or Bob Dylan. Sample a soothing spiritual CD called, *Secret Garden*, sung by the Norwegian/Celtic duo of Fionnula Sherry and Rolf Lovland. Let the music calm the souls of the group. If by chance the gals are requesting something a little more upbeat then rock out with Jai Uttal.

Color

Purple will pump some purity into the kitchen. This is the dinner to become a fairy princess or priestess in shades of purple. Why do we only dress up as fairies at Halloween? Well, not tonight. Go ahead gals get pretty in purple and celebrate an unearthly kingdom with lots of scarves and silky fabrics. Wear a pair of soft wide bottom velvet pants with a silk off the shoulder pink blouse and a periwinkle lace undershirt. If the night spells complete comfort, slip into a pair of soft yoga pants, purple Ugg boots and a playful ball cap.

Essential oil

Oils to have on hand are jasmine, peppermint, spearmint, peace and calm and white angelica. Place peppermint on the bottom of the feet to provide a little more energy for the evening, then smell pretty with a couple drops of jasmine behind the ear.

Closing

Create a secret handshake and use it to seal the group's intuitive powers. Then offer each other a loving hand in friendship and other-worldly senses. Honor the little witch within and never share this sacred handshake with anyone outside this soul sisterhood community.

After party ritual

Right before bed give yourself a head massage, especially around the temples. Place peace and calm essential oil in your hands—rub together and inhale the sweet aroma. Position your hands to the sides of your ears. Relax. Feel good and have a moment without thinking about anything. Trust that life is working out for your highest and best good.

Conscious fortune cookie says:

A woman who is open to equally feeling with her heart and thinking with her head will never struggle through life.

The Seventh Party: Live Joy

Overview

Aspiritual connection reveals a higher vibration of joy. At dinner have each gal recite a joyful prayer while sipping on a cocktail made of lemons, limes, pomegranate juice, blue agave and one drop of the essential oil of lavender. Blend this mixture with a few frozen organic strawberries and garnish the slushy drink with a sprig of fresh rosemary.

Start the evening off with cheerful sautéed crab cakes accompanied with a chipotle sauce. Make a joyful noise into the world by serving a main plate of black rice pasta noodles topped with organic shrimp, Shakti mushrooms, fresh spinach pesto doused in

olive oil, garlic, soy sauce and rice wine. Yum! Have plenty of grated Parmigiano-Reggiano on hand to baptize the dish. Celebrate the evening by serving the famous tofu birthday cake. This is the party to birth a new you. Honor a greater force within and rejoice to a real spiritual night out with the girls. Happy Spiritual Birthday!

During this party have the gals wear white turbans, white ball caps or go to an antique store and discover vintage white hats to celebrate a sophisticated but heavenly event. The dinner table is covered with white: linens, candles, lilies and angel feathers. Light up the room with 20-30 white candles and pretend you forgot to pay the electric bill—no overhead lights. Create an imaginative night to remember.

Sample Menu

Fresh-Squeezed Lavender Slush
A Garnish of fresh Rosemary

Sautéed Crab Cakes topped with Homemade
Chipotle Sauce & Lamb Leaf

Fresh Spinach Pesto Tossed with Black Rice
Noodles & Shakti Mushrooms
Organic Shrimp
Parmigiano-Reggiano & Fresh Spinach Leaves

Tofu Birthday Cake with Chocolate Ganache Sauce
Flax Seed Apple Pie

Jasmine tea

Recipe for Tofu Birthday Cake

Ingredients

2 ¼ cups of oat flour
2 teaspoons baking powder
½ teaspoon sea salt
1¼ cups of sucanat sugar
½ cup butter—room temperature

8 ounces soft tofu
1½ cups soymilk
2 teaspoons vanilla
½ cup strawberry jam
1 pint fresh strawberries, thinly sliced

Preparation

Preheat oven to 350 degrees Fahrenheit (175 degrees Celsius). Grease two 8-inch cake pans. In a large bowl, combine flour, baking powder and sea salt. Set aside.

In another bowl, mix sugar and butter until creamy. In a food processor or blender, mix tofu, soymilk and vanilla until smooth. Add sugar mixture to tofu then add to dry ingredients. Pour into pans and bake for 30 minutes.

Cool the cakes then place on the bottom layer strawberry jam and sliced berries. Place the second cake on top and drizzle with a chocolate ganache sauce.

Ganache frosting

Ingredients

1 cup of heavy cream or soymilk
1 package of semisweet chocolate chips

Preparation

Combine liquid with the chips in a double boiler and melt. Stir until fully melted and smooth. Drizzle chocolate in the middle of cake and let it drip down the sides.

Conscious life lessons

The conscious life lesson for this gathering is to discuss feelings of joy and how it may appear in life. How can more conscious joy be brought into each precious moment? How can we learn to be grateful for what we have instead of whining and focusing on what is missing in our lives? Remember once disconnected from source, God or infinite power, all joy will be lost. Practice making G-O-D and J-O-Y safe three letter words and speak them often from the heart to friends and family.

Create a spiritual path: The word G-O-D when broken down will help us better understand how to create a personal spiritual path. The G represents generate or get the job done. This means go out and make life happen in a healthy, solid and grounded way. The O represents the wait, the letting go, the flow, the trust or the spiritual faith in the pause. The D represents delivery or the manifestation. Over time, we learn to detach from the outcome as the process begins again.

The G-O-D method is continually occurring throughout our lives, every moment of every day. Women who have become boldly masculine and too earth bound have a very hard time accepting the O or passively allowing a magical flow into life. They become distracted with the *doing* and the *getting* instead of the *allowing* and *being*. There seems to be limited space for a passive pause and spiritual energy in our world these days. To be healthy and whole women, we must learn to nurture our spiritual nature and recapture the faith and trust in the flow. How do we truly know God and a spiritual path? Do the interpersonal work, then slow down, clear the mind, feel a strong spiritual connection within, stay focused and increase the faith. Discuss this concept with the group.

Strengths

The well-adjusted woman is detached from the ego self. She truly knows how to be in this world in a powerful and grounded way. She has learned to honor all aspects (higher and lower) of herself because both are blessings and always reside within her. She knows at the end of the day she has reincarnated to play out a divine role. She is not consumed with sorrow or worry. She understands that in the human experience nothing is so-called perfect or everlasting. This woman honors the revered sacraments of marriage and motherhood, and she is committed to her duties. Samadhi or the union between the self and God are primary to all her relationships. She is clever at balancing a confident, earthly lifestyle with a relaxed spiritual connection.

Weaknesses

The lower aspect will appear in this woman when she tries to cheat life and all that goes along with joyful living. She doesn't have time for ritual, sacred connection or the taste for bliss. Unfortunately, this woman tends to be caught up in worldly possessions and this is where she keeps her focus, even at the cost of losing the people she loves. Honesty and integrity are missing from this gal's life. She has no problem lying to friends and herself. There will be much hesitation for this woman to trust and believe in the Divine Creator. She lacks faith because she is distracted with worldly affairs. Instead of living with spiritual highs, she escapes her earthly experiences with harmful addictions and distractions.

Go around the room and speak candidly on the strengths and weaknesses mentioned above. Share with the other girls any personal traits.

Healing ritual

Create a ritual where the girls take turns and step into a sacred healing circle. The person encircled will listen to what the other girls have to say about her character. **Warning**—be gentle and honest girlfriends. Let the women from outside the circle be a conduit for channeling God's love, light and cheerful words.

If the above ritual is too challenging, another idea is to research favorite crystals and discuss each stone's healing properties. Invite a gemologist to dinner to share her love and knowledge. Discuss how gemstones can be used for healing the mind, body and soul.

Before meditation, take both hands to the top of the head and begin to pull the fingers downward toward the neck, as if to divide the skull in half. Create an imaginary opening in the top of the head. This process stimulates the energy that often gets stuck in the crown and blocks spiritual vigor.

Meditation

Meditate on Samadhi and connect with a sacred light. With closed eyes, individually establish a strong link and ask the spirit guides to identify your conscious contribution to this planet. How will a conscious life play out, and what changes are to be made to your current state of affairs? Have each woman write her contribution down on a piece of paper and store in a safe place. Make sure to call in the angelic realm while meditating.

Music

The musical note of B is the vibration for this party. Do some research on angelic music and bring in the sounds from heaven. Here are a few albums to consider: *Soaring with Angels*, healing angelic music channeled by Frederic Delarue, *Liquid Bells*, sounds of crystal bowl healing by Damien Rose and *All is forgiven,* a sweet spiritual hymn by Ashana. The above music will put you immediately into a higher frequency. End the party by listening to the popular Gayatri mantra and find the joy.

Color

White: Go for the all-white look and turn your house into heaven. Don't panic, not all skin tones can wear pure white so try to include a warm cream. A cozy oversized lambswool sweater with crop cotton slacks could be one option for the night. Look through the closet and pull out everything white or cream—lace, leather and linen. Make sure to add a large vintage brooch to complete the look. Invite the angelic world into the dressing room for this debut. Attention eclectic gal: Don't forget to put on a pair of old white Converse tennis shoes or white lace up boots to finish the look.

Essential oil

Lotus, spruce, joy, Palo Santo and helichrysum are the oils for the evening. The oil of joy is Young Living's exclusive blended oil that offers a sweet attractive fragrance. Joy oil offers a high vibration and can be placed directly on the body. Use this oil as a daily signature perfume and set an intention to always be joyful.

Closing

In the sacred circle have each girlfriend envision an imaginary halo over her head. Take a deep inhale and connect with the spirit realm and on the exhale breath, have everyone bring her halo slowly down around the body, past the head, neck, chest and all the way to the feet.

Put closure to the night with a candle ceremony. The hostess will make sure all the girls have a small candle. She will first light her candle. The girl standing next to her will then tilt her unlit candle to the flame. Continue this ritual until all candles are glowing. *The hostess may decide to use candles throughout the house that have already been burning, but be careful of the melted wax.* When all the candles are aglow have girlfriends visually connect one by one with each other, say a group prayer and then together blow out the candles and say goodnight. Set an intention to live daily with a joyful heart, mind and soul.

After party ritual

How can more magic and joy be brought into life? What will a new personal conscious life look like in a day, week or year? Specifically, what is your conscious contribution to this planet? Write and reflect. Place the writings in a secure place and someday revisit them.

Conscious fortune cookie says:

A woman who believes in or knows GOD will find bliss and live a complete life of JOY.

THE EIGHTH PARTY: 1ˢᵗ MYSTERY DINNER

R eflect upon the seven parties. Which dinner has affected you most deeply and why? Create the mystery dinner using the elements from that party or choose several parties. Be able to share with the group the reasoning behind your design.

Overview _____

Conscious life lesson _____

Strengths _____

Weaknesses _____

Healing rituals _____

Meditation-neutral _____

Music _____

Color _____

Essential oil _____

Closing _____

After party ritual _____

Conscious fortune cookie says _____

We have individual character traits in all seven parties and it is very important to acknowledge each of these strengths and weaknesses and how they have touched our lives. With conscious consideration, we start to notice that one group of traits seems to be a theme that keeps replaying in our lives. There will be one party that is intensely appropriate to our life's journey. It will fit perfectly, like an expensive leather glove. We each have an individual blood type, fingerprint and horoscope sign, right? Why not consider that our soul has picked a dominant energy source and uses it to teach us our lessons and aid our personal progress? Use this mystery party to determine who you are and what your life purpose is.

An Example: Out of all the party themes or lessons, let's say the fifth party really speaks to you. Snicker. There seems to be a real teacher inside, and unfortunately it has not manifested itself. You have not found your voice. Think about some of the aspects, either weaknesses or strengths, that support you or get in your way. Maybe the concept of being grounded is a concern. Allow time to reflect upon this notion. Ask yourself, why it is so hard to stay grounded? It is time to move forward on your trusted journey.

It might be interesting to bring in a hypnotherapist and after dinner go through a session with this professional in front of your peers. Go to your core and ask for clarification. If you feel stuck, trust that other soul sisters may feel the same way.

Another idea is to bring in an educator you admire and have her share her sacred journey with the group of gals. Ask her specifically to address tips on staying focused and grounded. Her life's story will most likely shine some light on your own path and provide helpful insights. Be open to becoming the powerful teacher.

Introspection and reflection are key words that emanate from this mystery party. Learn to properly honor these levels of consciousness. Take off the mask and use this party to reflect upon your reason for being.

THE NINTH PARTY: 2ND MYSTERY DINNER

Meditate on the perfect conscious dinner. Go into a deep state Samadhi, and when a strong connection has been established ask God, spirit guides, angels or a higher self to provide the details for the perfect conscious party. Trust what you hear then get busy and create the 2nd mystery dinner. A message will be provided by the spirit world—trust. It is time to take a leap of faith and be prepared to share the magic with the group.

Overview _____

Conscious life lesson _____

Strengths _____

Weaknesses _____

Healing rituals _____

Meditation-neutral _____

Music _____

Color _____

Essential oil _____

Closing _____

After party ritual _____

Conscious fortune cookie says _____

True consciousness comes when we are able to get beyond the noise in our heads. We are able to connect with an inner knowingness and God. Intuition is available to all of us and we don't have to meditate 20 years while sitting crossed-legged in a cave in Northern India. Some of us might have had a clear connection when we were very young and have grown into sensitive, intuitive ladies who have no problem honoring an inner knowingness.

As grown women, the wise crone appears to have a deep appreciation and a clear link to this unknown phenomenon. Over time, spiritual practices like yoga, Tai Chi and meditation have helped develop this connection. Some of us have gotten very trusting and cozy with the spirit world. We hear voices from our angelic guides that stimulate a conversation. Some of us have a keen sense of what is going to happen next. We see spirits, angels and dead relatives. We may even call ourselves psychics or mediums.

However, don't get too attached to feeling special and glamorize this notion, because it is forever fleeting. One day voices will come through as clear as if someone from the spirit realm was standing behind whispering in your ear the answers to your every prayer, only to be followed the next day—by nothing. Keep all expectations in balance and just learn to receive what has been provided without trying to personalize it.

In these present times, it is no longer scary to use words like: witch, psychic, spiritual healing, clairsentient, power of the third eye and God centeredness. We are living in a changing time where we are all shifting into a new vibration, using fresh choices of words and accepting different beliefs. This is part of the universal growth that the planet must go through. We are expected to expand our horizons and be more understanding of others and their belief systems.

An example: The hardest part of this exercise is to learn to trust what you hear and imagine. Let's say you connected with the 6th and 7th parties in a profound way and in meditation, thoughts around these parties keep coming up. You begin to notice in your meditations, visions of a church. The meditations are taking you back to your childhood days and Sunday's church school. All of a sudden you get the notion to call your pastor. During the phone call you mention the *Conscious Dinner Parties* and the pastor loves the idea of a conscious event and invites your group for a private church meditation. Maybe the church has a Parish house that is attached to the grounds and possibly an ideal place to host a simple dinner. Okay, a bit quirky—but could be an amazing night out with your friends and it all came from listening to the thoughts in meditation or aha moments while doing the dishes or yoga. The little signs that pop into our heads are precious and are importance messages from our souls.

Prizes and Awards

At the last mystery party, take a moment and pass around the hat. Three gifts (awards) will be decided upon and purchased for the grand finale. Assign one woman to be responsible who will gladly purchase the prizes and have them available for the final party. It will be up to the group to decide upon the donations then set a date, time and location to rejoice.

When the time comes, uncork the champagne and celebrate all the conscious successes. Pick a favorite restaurant and meet there. As a group, choose three women who will be the winners. Vote for the women who had gusto and gave 100% to make this conscious project a success.

The first prize goes to the most conscious contributor. The second prize is awarded to most notably improved, and the third prize is offered to the gal who hosted the best house party.

First prize:	The Queen of Consciousness
Second prize:	The Princess of Enlightenment
Third prize:	The Angelic Being

Award gifts:

Here are a few suggestions for gift ideas:

- A gift certificate for a favorite spa experience
- A framed certificate with soul sisters' signatures
- A bouquet of flowers
- Gemstone bracelets or necklaces

- *Sacred Sisterhood* printed T-shirts
- Essential oils
- An angel or fairy book
- A meditation shawl
- Scented candles
- A Feng Shui consultation
- Music-mp3 of all the songs from the parties
- *Conscious Dinner Parties* monogram aprons

- _____
- _____
- _____

PART III

Reflections

Party with a Purpose

When women reflect back over their lifetimes, they find themselves reviewing stages of life—inner child, rebellious teenager, wild goddess, sacred motherhood and the wise elder. Choices have been made, either consciously or unconsciously, during each of these phases that set life on its course. Along the way, our choices lead us to experience a variety of emotions from joy to pain. We discover that everything in life is temporary and even painful situations pass.

It becomes our job no matter where we are in our journey to stay focused and find the joy. Our conscious paths reflect our attitudes and willingness to learn the lessons and move forward with a spiritual pep in our step. At the end of life, we will look back and say, "Yep, I was conscious, had a great time, learned what I needed to know, shifted some karma and completed the job my soul was sent to do."

The masses are awakening to a new vibration and great changes. Right now the mainstream population is still consumed with outside influences, like how to make more money, be more powerful, economic trends, political affairs, worldly viewpoints and consumerism. Spiritual growth is not a priority in many people's lives. However, the fate of the world depends on the courage to awaken. Spiritual clarity is vital.

There is a small percentage of the population who actually spends time praying, meditating and honoring spiritual rituals. These souls understand their mission is to support the greater good. Light workers need to ground their energies so their labors can be felt and changes made. The G-O-D principal must be implemented to encourage the feminine energy back into the world. The time has come for the spiritual minorities to make their move to help the masses progress to a higher frequency. Everyone must honor the changes that are occurring on the planet and seek balance in all affairs. As the saying goes, "love straight from the heart pulls us together, never apart."

Inspiration means *in spirit.* When we are in spirit, the universal flow of pure consciousness is upon us. It's time to manifest wants, needs or simply what we spend our time thinking about. There will be peaks and valleys in this flow, but stepping out of our troubles becomes much easier and quicker as we look for the next moment of inspiration. We now truly author the details of a brilliant life story and our goal is to know a peaceful, inner spiritual realm as we live a powerful life here on earth.

We have discovered that *Conscious Dinner Parties* have offered us the chance to get inspired as we took our turn creating a sacred event. Rituals afforded us the opportunities to know ourselves and our true friends a bit better. Girlfriends have learned to stay conscious minute by minute and to turn this task into a key life strategy. We remain empowered and acknowledge our strengths, instead of drifting away on a daunting sea of weaknesses. It is now time to anchor our boats to a neutral dock of peacefulness as we embrace the power of daily meditation.

A real teacher is a friend who can love and show compassion. Some women come by this naturally, while others must work to stay positive and keep childhood dramas and strong egos at a distance. From time to time, we will have to become the teacher and the student. Each role helps us in many different ways to create the wholeness we seek.

With any luck, the parties have cultivated a strong unbreakable girlfriend bond. Still, at times girlfriends can disappear from our lives. Dramas will happen and so will breakups. They are part of the human experience sprinkled with a little karma. Notice when there is an intense connection upon meeting someone new. This energetic pull is introducing a soul mate into our life. This bond offers a mirror reflection into our own reality. Is this friendship a test? Have old life lessons been cleared from the auric field or is this a reminder there is still more work to be done? In either case, treat those relationships with care until it becomes clear whether this is a longstanding association. If parting company soon becomes the only resolution, remember, no dramas and mentally say to yourself, "I am sorry my friend. As we go our separate ways, know that I will always love you."

Cherish the times shared at the dinner parties. Compare some of these conscious parties to past dining affairs of drinking and eating too much with limited spiritual attention. Notice how the energy is different simply because clear conscious intentions have been set. This might be a sign to shift from the old unconscious gatherings to full-blown regular sacred soirees. Embrace the conscious life lessons and healing rituals. Learn to take a risk and share a conscious event. Help others transition old behaviors into exciting new age modes. Teach mindfulness to everyone you meet and be an example out into the neighborhood.

THE BIG SECRET

There is a Metaphysical mystery behind the effectiveness of these parties. Portals of energy systems, known as chakras, flow around and through our bodies, touching us in a magnificent way. The parties have been carefully designed to profoundly affect this energy flow by opening higher levels of consciousness within us. Major life modifications can occur by healing and balancing these gateways. Unbeknownst to the dinner guests, their energies are able to take a psychic relationship to friends and the spiritual intentions formulated by each of the nine events. The outcome is a physical, spiritual, emotional and mental healing which results in a very impressive shift in consciousness. Remember, it just takes one person's energy to shift for the world to change.

Every action creates a reaction. We are all interconnected through our thoughts, feelings and actions. Conscious life lessons have taught us well. We now get to choose from what we have learned to live a full and happy life. Whether a woman leads with her strengths or weaknesses it will be her choice. This decision is extremely important and in the end will influence the collective consciousness.

A final thought as we end our journey together—start each and every day with a conscious contribution. We have discussed several in the book: meditate, pray, formulate a spiritual ritual, create strong bonds with conscious friends, exercise, eat sustainable foods, cook with essential oils, listen to uplifting music, think green, be passionate and help the planet move to a higher vibration—one conscious girlfriend at a time.

Refer back to this book and don't forget all the heartwarming pleasures from the parties. Keep these memories alive in your spirit. Be available to your soul sisters during both joyful and difficult times. Share more compassion when times of imbalance, fears and uncertainties show up—and they are guaranteed to appear. In the end, be grateful for all your conscious girlfriends to save the day.

A wise teacher and close friend of mine wrote:

"It is time to know our value. Every human being can serve as the womb to birth a new world. It is important to understand the magnitude of what is happening and our role in the evolutionary process. Each of us is being given an opportunity to make our contribution and to participate in our own special way. As we do so, we will realize our value and get to know our true essence at a very profound level."

Guru Rattana, Ph.D. www.yogatech.com

Gratitude goes out to all my teachers and girlfriends. They have taught me well.
Namaste

REFERENCES:
BOOKS, ARTICLES & WEBSITES

"Consciousness," in the Stanford Encyclopedia of Philosophy

Eye of the Lotus, Psychology of the Chakras by Richard Jelusich

Rieki Self-Healing by Dr. Mikao Usui

Essays of World Religions by Houston Smith

The Gift of Womanhood by Guru Rattana, Ph.D.

The Kundalini Yoga Experience by Guru Dharam Khalsa & Darryl O'Keeffe

Eight Limbs, The Yoga Suttras of Patanjali

Vegetarian, the Taste of South India by Manju Rahim & Salimi Pushpanath

"Consciousness" in Webster's Dictionary

What's Cooking Within by www.jylauxter.com

Young Living Essential Oils www.youngliving.com

Other books and products by the author:

What's Cooking Within? Yoga, Meditation and Recipes

Get High On A Higher Vibration, A Tune-Up for Conscious Living

Yoga DVDs:

Healing Yoga

Desert Gentle Yoga

Guided Meditation CD:

Sacred Healing Meditation with Voices of Angels

For more information on Jyl's international workshops, retreats, healing sessions and conscious parties, email ylauxter@aol.com & www.jylauxter.com.

Lightning Source UK Ltd.
Milton Keynes UK
UKOW05n1834300714

236049UK00001B/10/P